ROCK CHORD RIFFS

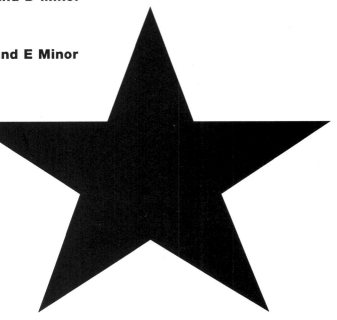

Exclusive Distributors:
Music Sales Limited
8/9 Frith Street, London W1V 5TZ, England.
Music Sales Pty Limited
120 Rothschild Avenue, Rosebery, NSW 2018, Australia.
Music Sales Corporation
257 Park Avenue South, New York, NY10010, United States of America.

Order No. AM90237
ISBN 0-7119-3300-6
This book © Copyright 1996 by Wise Publications.

Unauthorised reproduction of any part of this publication by any
means including photocopying is an infringement of copyright.

Book design by Niche.
Cover design by Michael Bell Design.
Cover photography by George Taylor.
Text photographs courtesy of London Features International.
Edited by Pat Conway.
Music processed by Seton Music Graphics.

Your Guarantee of Quality:
As publishers, we strive to produce every book to
the highest commercial standards.
The music has been freshly engraved and this book has
been carefully designed to make playing from it a real pleasure.
Throughout, the printing and binding have been
planned to ensure a sturdy, attractive publication which
should give years of enjoyment.
If your copy fails to meet our high standards, please
inform us and we will gladly replace it.

Music Sales' complete catalogue describes
thousands of titles and is available in full colour sections
by subject, direct from Music Sales Limited.
Please state your areas of interest and send a
cheque/postal order for £1.50 for postage to:
Music Sales Limited, Newmarket Road, Bury St. Edmunds, Suffolk IP33 3YB.

Wise Publications

London / New York / Paris / Sydney / Copenhagen / Madrid

Printed in the United Kingdom by
Caligraving Limited Thetford Norfolk

HOW TO USE THIS BOOK

This book features 50 different chord riffs (progressions) which are independent of each other. Each "Chord Riff" contains the chord patterns used, the order in which they are played and whether they are strummed or plucked.
This is written on the "Rhythm & Sequence Track".

RHYTHM & SEQUENCE TRACK

The rhythm & sequence track is written in tablature form (each line represents a string). The numbers ① ② ③ written above the rhythm and sequence track indicate a particular version of the chord to be played.

CHORD RIFF EXERCISE

For this exercise simply strum each chord down and up to a count of four. The ↑ indicates a downward strum and the ↓ indicates an upward strum. Use a pick (or plectrum) to strum.

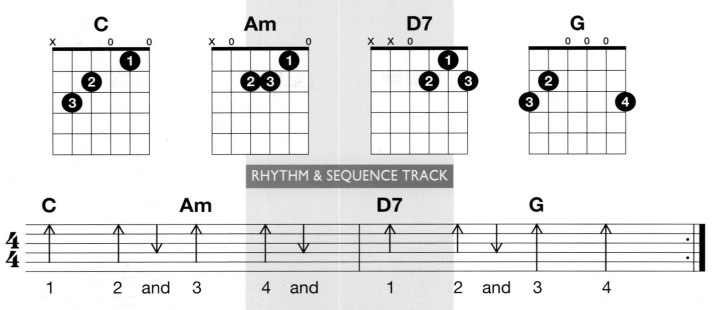

RHYTHM & SEQUENCE TRACK

As well as strumming chords, the individual notes of a chord can be struck with the pick or played with thumb and fingers

A ⊓ above the note means strike down with the pick.
A ∨ above the note means strike up with the pick.

t   above (or below) the note means thumb
i   above (or below) the note means index finger
m   above (or below) the note means middle finger
a   above (or below) the note means ring finger.

POWER CHORD RIFF IN

POWER ROCK

1

Listen to the accents = > on the first beat/between beats two and three/ and fourth beat of each bar = >

Asus4

Bar =
(Example here shows bar one)

$\frac{4}{4}$

1   and   2   and   3   and   4

Accent Symbol = >

These accents tend to make things more powerful and percussive.
Try experimenting with other accents to create different rhythms.

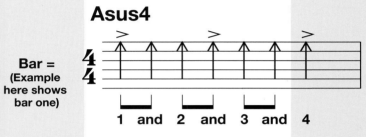

Asus4   X 0   0   **A**   X 0   0   **Esus4**   0   0 0   **E**   0   0 0

RHYTHM & SEQUENCE TRACK

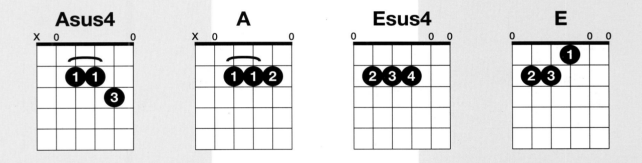

Asus4   **A**   **Esus4**

$\frac{4}{4}$

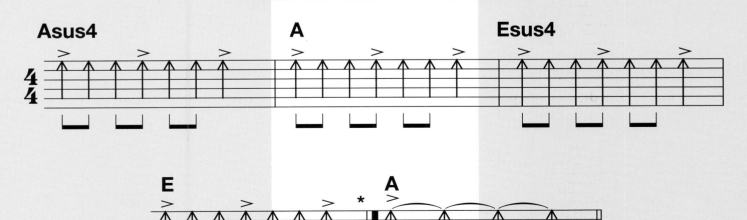

E   **A**

* Go back to the start of this sequence and play it again.

2

A♭

This is quite easy really,
however, after the C chord at
the end of the third measure,
keep your first finger 'barred'
across the 4th, 3rd and 2nd
strings when you play the F❷
chord. You will see why when
you play the riff.

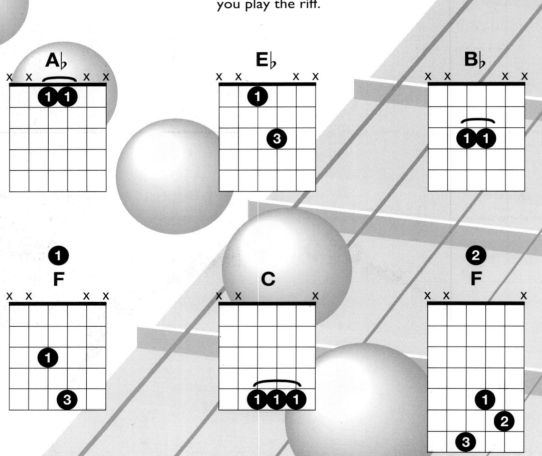

3

The rhythm for this chord riff is =

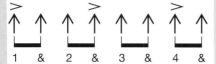

1   &   2   &   3   &   4   &

Just use downstrokes throughout,
it is the accents that make the rhythm.

Am   **Open strings**   **C**

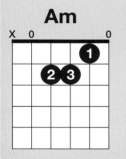 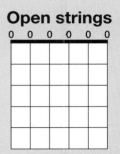 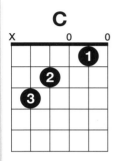

G   **F**

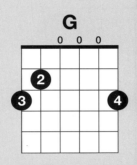 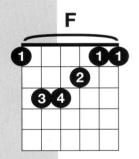

BRUCE SPRINGSTEEN

RHYTHM & SEQUENCE TRACK

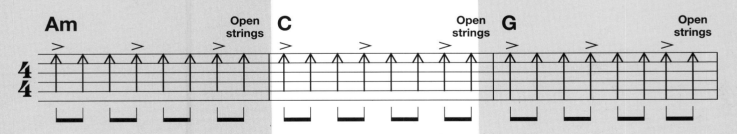

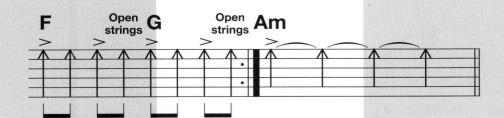

FUNKY ROCK CHORD RIFF IN

4

FUNK/ROCK

There's a lot of rhythm content in this one and it really would be impossible to write down exactly how I play this on the recording but here is the basic rhythm laid out for you.

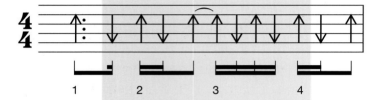

A7
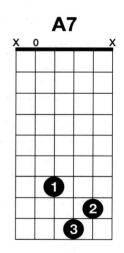

D/A
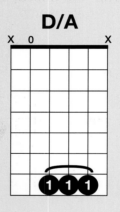

Am7
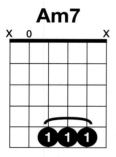

RHYTHM & SEQUENCE TRACK

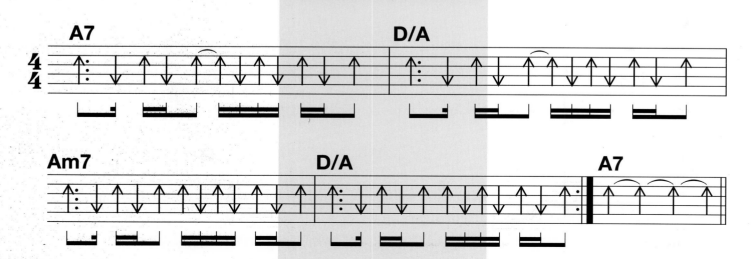

ROCK CHORD RIFF IN

5

Try the following rhythm exercise before attempting the chord riff. I think you will find it beneficial for the rhythm that is needed here.

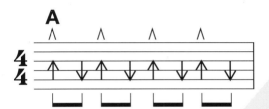

Hit the strings with the palm of the right-hand at the bridge as you strum the chord, this will create a 'percussive' sound.

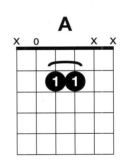

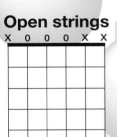

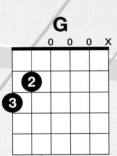

RHYTHM & SEQUENCE TRACK

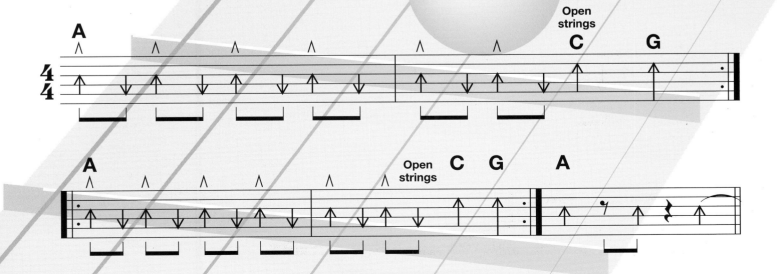

ROCK INTRO CHORD RIFF IN

6

ROCK

I've used this brilliant little rocker on lots of gigs, it's full of impact and very easy to play. Bend the strings down slightly with your first fingers on the second chord to create an authentic 'rock' effect.

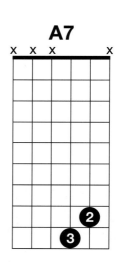

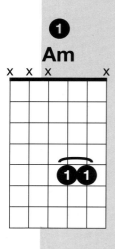

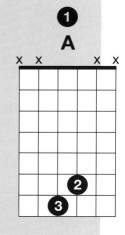

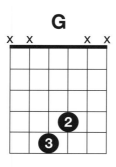

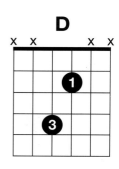

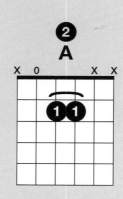

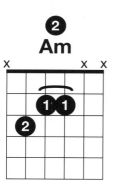

RHYTHM & SEQUENCE TRACK

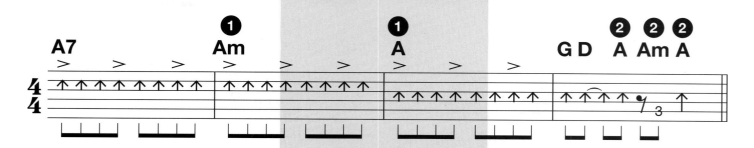

8

There are quite a few two-note chords here. The first chord will have more impact if you can 'slide' onto it.

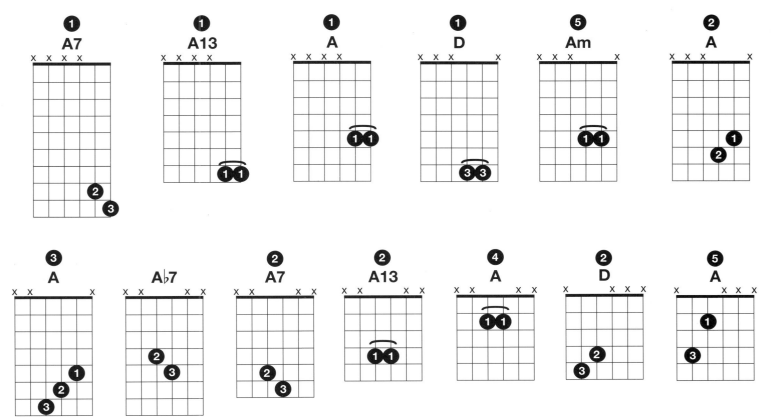

RHYTHM & SEQUENCE TRACK

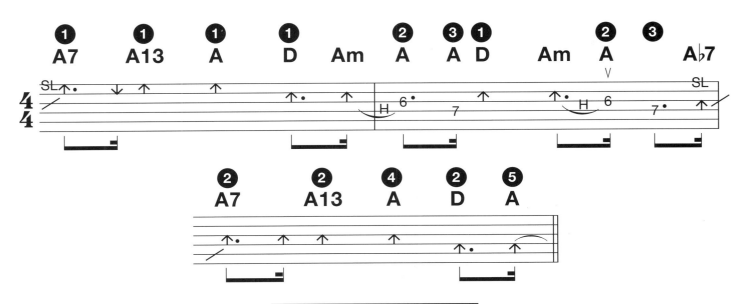

CONTEMPORARY CHORD RIFF IN A

The three chords used here, A, E and D were used extensively in the fifties (most notably by Buddy Holly, Eddie Cochran, Everly Brothers, etc.) They are still popular today in the repertoires of even the most modern artistes.

A   E   D

RHYTHM & SEQUENCE TRACK

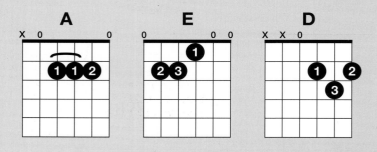

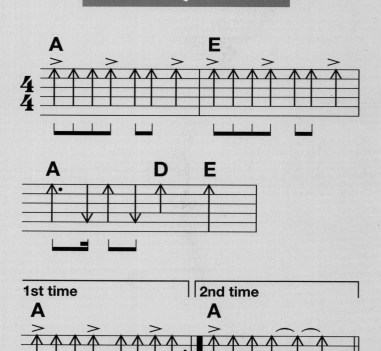

ROCK CHORD RIFF IN A

PICK & FINGERS

An interesting feature that's used here is the combined use of the pick and fingers to sound the notes. Try to damp the 5th string throughout with the palm of your hand over the bridge saddle.

A   A6

RHYTHM & SEQUENCE TRACK

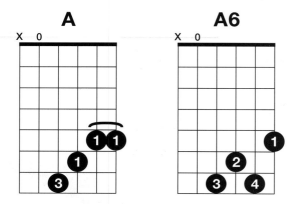

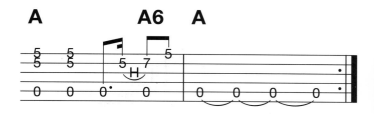

POWER ROCK

A 'percussive' effect is achieved by 'choking' the strings. (X indicates the 'choked' strings). Stroke the strings with a pick but at the same time rest the edge of your palm (right-hand) against them. At the same time, release your left hand from the chord so your fingers just lie across the strings, ie. don't apply any pressure to the strings.

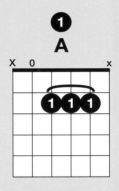

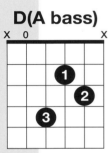

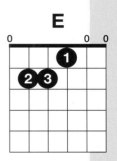

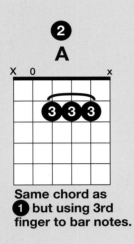

Same chord as ❶ but using 3rd finger to bar notes.

WHITESNAKE

RHYTHM & SEQUENCE TRACK

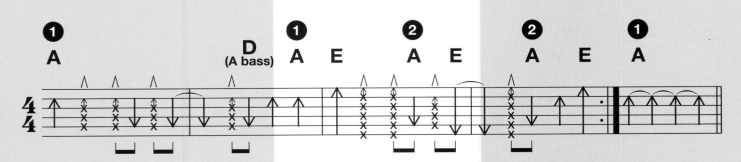

POWER CHORD RIFF IN

11

Play this tight and clean to obtain the most powerful impact.

POWER ROCK

GUNS N' ROSES

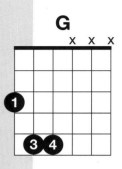

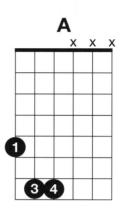

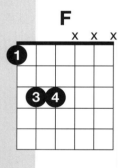

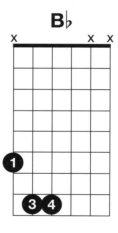

RHYTHM & SEQUENCE TRACK

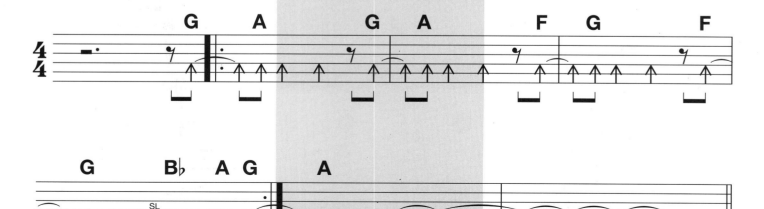

A
M I N O R

Here's a chord riff that really
moves along, it's a great vehicle
for the whole band to jam
along with.

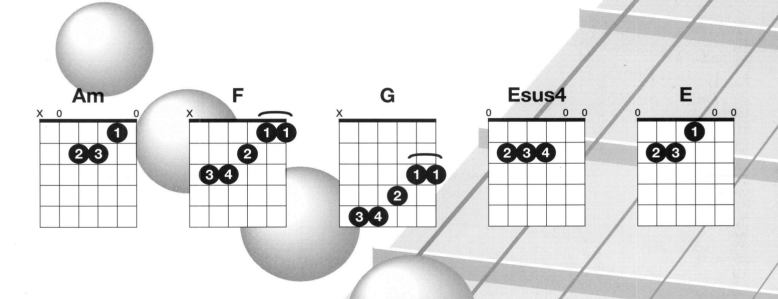

RHYTHM & SEQUENCE TRACK

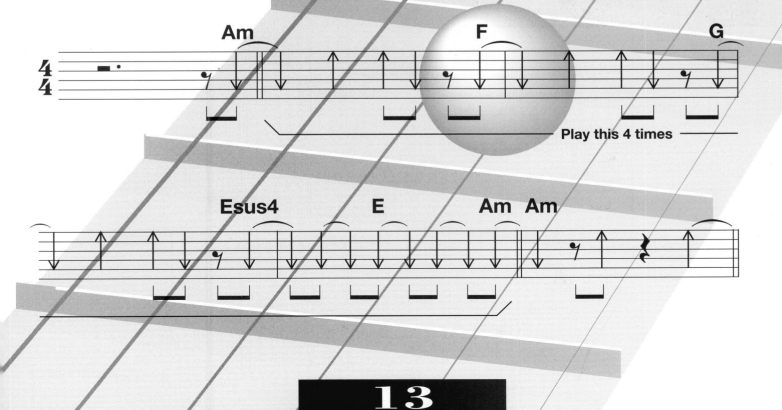

Play this 4 times

A pedal note can add excitement to an otherwise run-of-the-mill chord riff. You play the first chord and then retain the same root for the following chords.

①
A

E (A pedal)

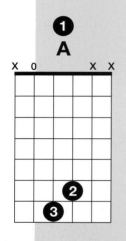

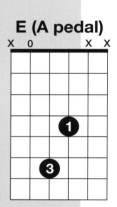

F#m (A pedal)

②
A

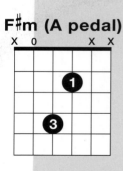

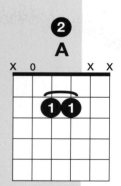

RHYTHM & SEQUENCE TRACK

①
A

E
(A pedal)

F#m
(A pedal)

E
(A pedal)

①
A

E
(A pedal)

F#m
(A pedal)

②
A

$\frac{4}{4}$

A

Here's a neat little rocker for you now using power chords. There are only three chords involved but there is a lot of chord changing.

G

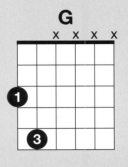

A

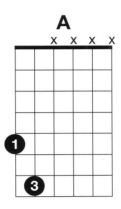

F

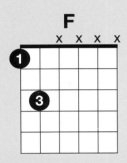

STATUS QUO

RHYTHM & SEQUENCE TRACK

15

Lots of energy is required here
so get out the glucose tablets!
Although a dirty amp setting is
preferable you will have to play
precisely, tightly and cleanly.
Lift your left-hand fingers off
slightly before each upstroke of
the A chord to create a
muted percussive effect .

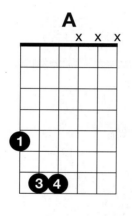

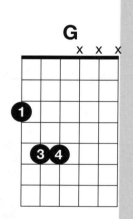

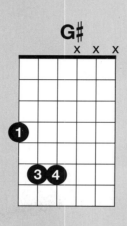

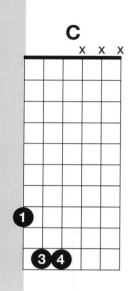

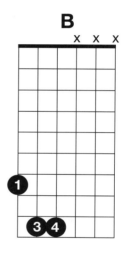

RHYTHM & SEQUENCE TRACK

Play this 4 times

16

This is played with a triplet feel throughout.

Damp the strings at the bridge for a chunky sound.

A
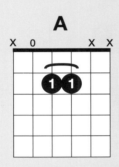

A7
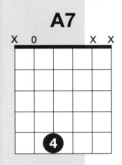

A6
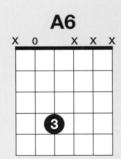

Aaug
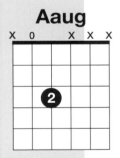

GARY MOORE

RHYTHM & SEQUENCE TRACK

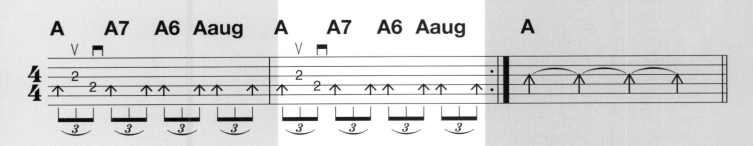

Try to play this with an acoustic guitar if possible, as this will add a more 'percussive' sort of sound. (Rather like the Everly Brothers style.)

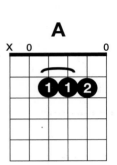

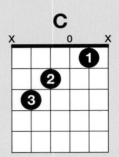

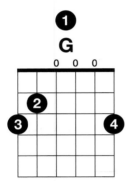

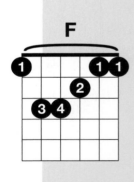

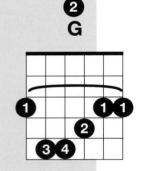

RHYTHM & SEQUENCE TRACK

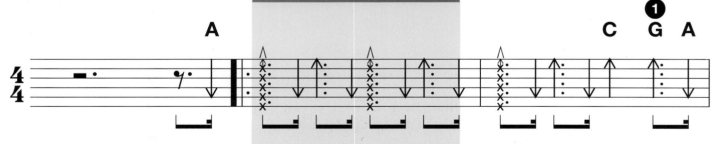

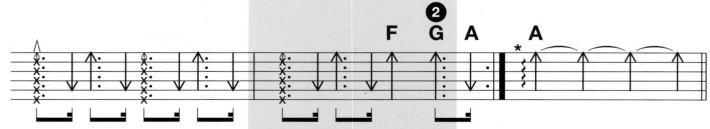

* = 'Sweep' Arpeggio (sweep strings down with the pick rather than strum).

A

You will need a dirty setting on the amp for this riff, but the chords must be hit cleanly to avoid any discordant notes.

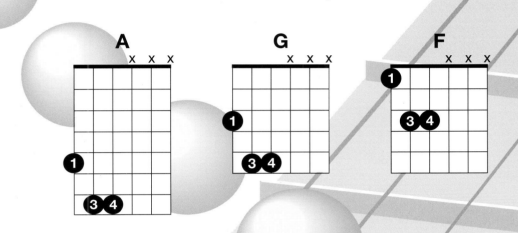

RHYTHM & SEQUENCE TRACK

ROCK 'n' ROLL CHORD RIFF IN

A.

TWO NOTE CHORDS

Try using this as a lead fill within a 12 bar rock'n'roll type of song. When you get to the C chord, drag the strings down slightly with the left-hand finger to create a string bend.

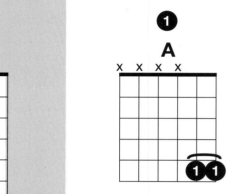

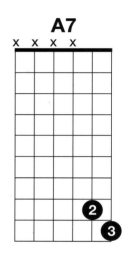

A7

A13

A

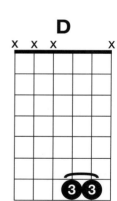

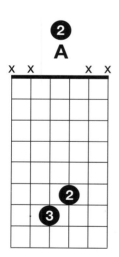

D

C

A

RHYTHM & SEQUENCE TRACK

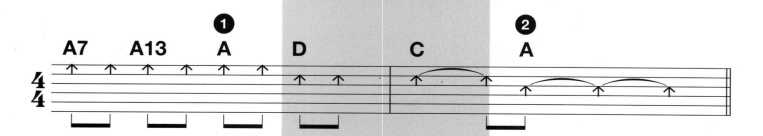

A7   A13   A   D   C   A

20

When 'barring' the A❷ chord with your 1st finger, be sure to arch it slightly so that it mutes the 1st string and keep this barré position for the next chord so that all you do is add the 2nd and 3rd fingers rather than changing the entire hand position.

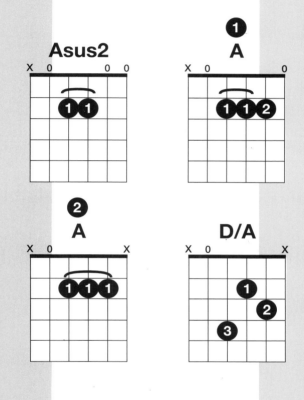

Asus2

A

A

D/A

RHYTHM & SEQUENCE TRACK

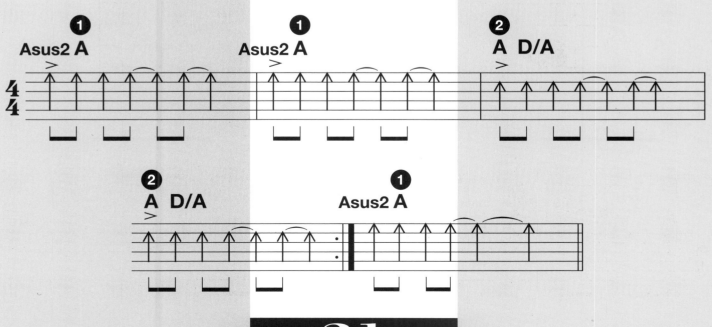

Using the open A & E strings as 'Pedal' notes throughout turns this otherwise ordinary 'A to Bm to C#m to Bm' chord riff into a much more exciting idea. There is an accent on the first, fourth and seventh strum of each bar.

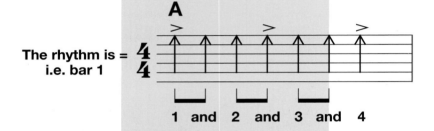

The rhythm is =
i.e. bar 1

1 and 2 and 3 and 4

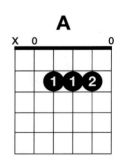

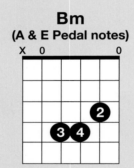

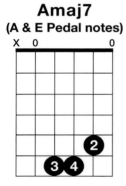

RHYTHM & SEQUENCE TRACK

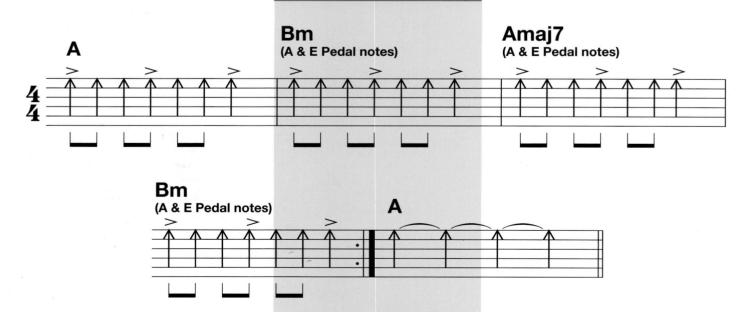

CHORD RIFF IN

Using a chorus/phaser/flanger
or similar effect and damping
the strings at the bridge will
give this a great sound.

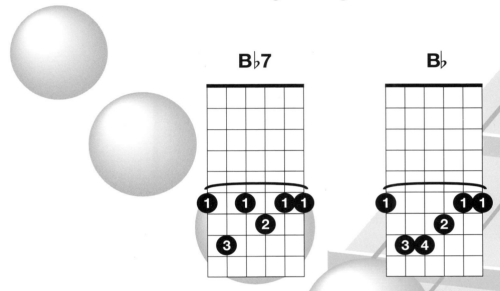

B♭7

B♭

RHYTHM & SEQUENCE TRACK

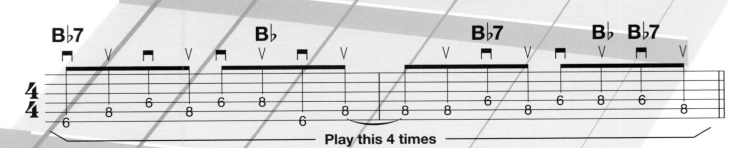

B♭7   **B♭**   **B♭7**   **B♭** **B♭7**

Play this 4 times

Accent the 1st, 4th and 7th
strum on each chord
throughout this riff.

BONNIE RAITT

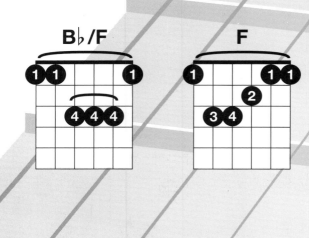

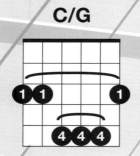

RHYTHM & SEQUENCE TRACK

B♭/F   F   B♭/F   C/G

Here's a powerful chord riff which shouldn't be too difficult to play. Notice that the third chord along is written as a D chord whilst the 4th, 3rd and 2nd strings are struck, but when the open E string is struck it then becomes an Dsus2 chord, notice also the slide from G to A (add D note) chords on the 4th measure.

B

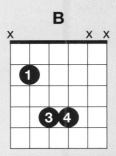

A

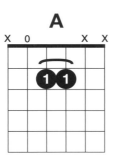

D (Becomes Dsus2 when open 1st string is struck)

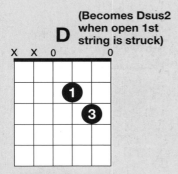

G

A (add D)

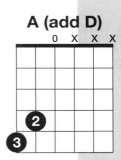

RHYTHM & SEQUENCE TRACK

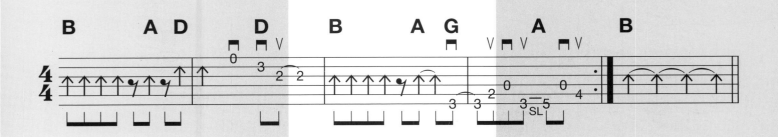

25

B MINOR

Keep this rhythmic, tight and solid throughout.
It is a great all purpose type of riff.

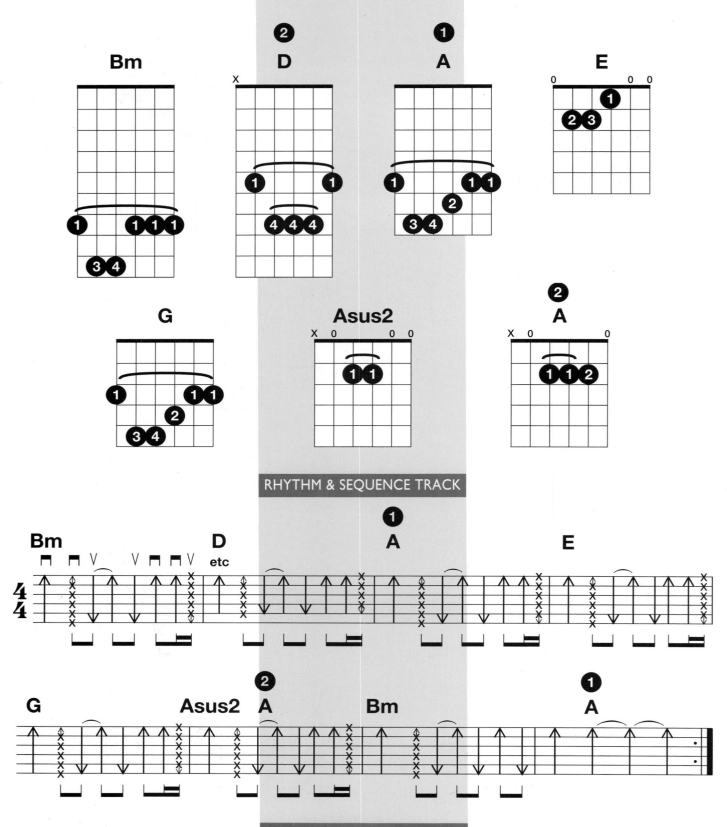

RHYTHM & SEQUENCE TRACK

This has a reggae feel throughout.

Bm7

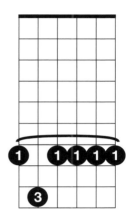

A

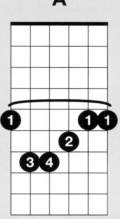

G

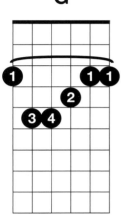

F♯m7

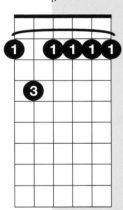

E

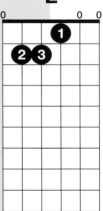

RHYTHM & SEQUENCE TRACK

Bm7　　　　**A**　　**G**　　　　　　**F♯m7**

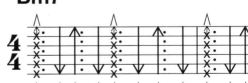
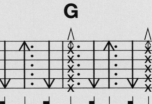
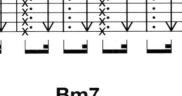

E　　　　**G**　　　　**A**　　　**Bm7**

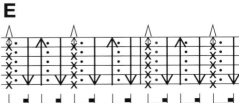
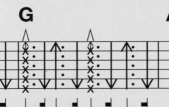
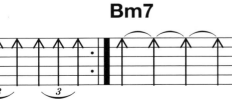

Start the rhythm with a
downstroke (choke the strings
with the palm of your hand
and lift your fingers off the
strings slightly). Here is an
idea of the rhythm.

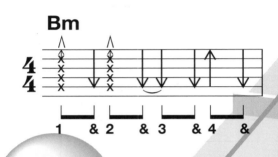

Bm

1 & 2 & 3 & 4 &

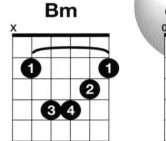

Bm

Open strings

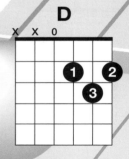

D

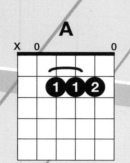

A

RHYTHM & SEQUENCE TRACK

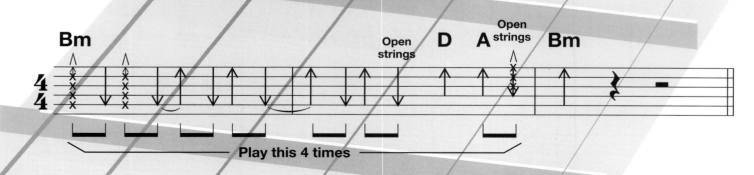

Bm ... **Open strings** **D** **A** **Open strings** **Bm**

Play this 4 times

C

Some chord riffs make use of 'chord scales'. Here I've used the C major scale where the notes are = C D E F G A B C. You will see I have indicated each scale note directly under the root note of each chord diagram.

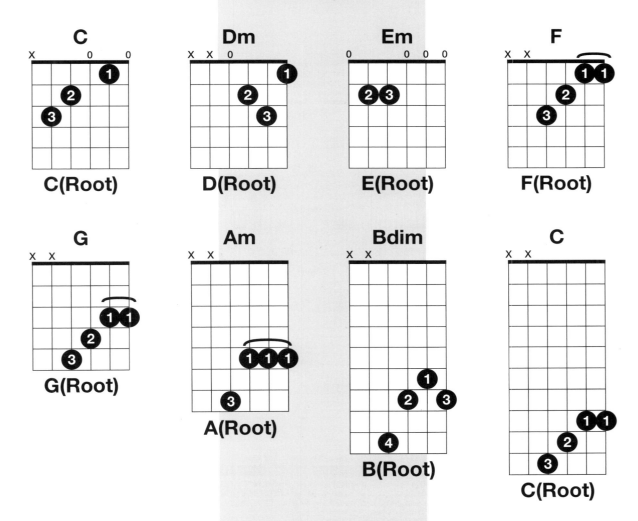

C
C(Root)

Dm
D(Root)

Em
E(Root)

F
F(Root)

G
G(Root)

Am
A(Root)

Bdim
B(Root)

C
C(Root)

RHYTHM & SEQUENCE TRACK

Use your thumb & fingers or pick & fingers to sound the notes from each chord.

C	Dm	Em	F	G	Am	Bdim	C
		0	1	3	5	7	8
1	3	0	1	3	5	6	8
0	2						
	0	2	3	5	7	9	10
3							

4/4

The first note of each chord acts as a 'falling bass line' throughout this classic arpeggio riff.

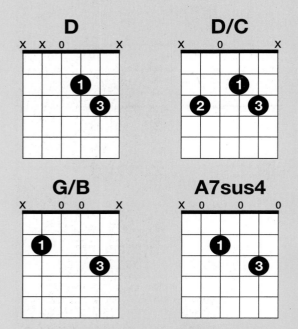

D   D/C

G/B   A7sus4

PEDAL NOTES

The accent = > on each chord plays an important part in creating this rhythm together with the otherwise straight forward eighth notes on the D pedal note played throughout.

D   F(D pedal note)   G(D pedal note)

RHYTHM & SEQUENCE TRACK

D   D7   G/B   A7sus4

Play this 4 times

D

RHYTHM & SEQUENCE TRACK

D   F(D pedal note)

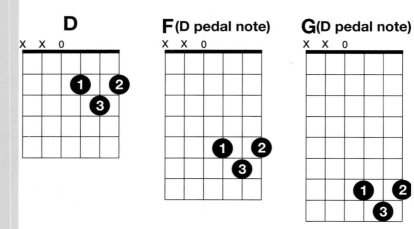

G(D pedal note)   D

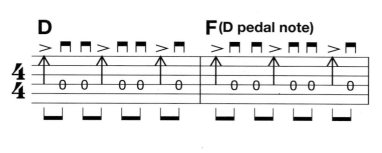
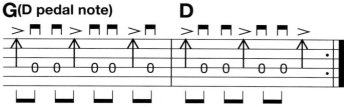

31

This chord riff uses 'barré' chords throughout. You'll notice on the C and B♭ diagrams the 2nd, 3rd and 4th strings are 'barréd' with the 4th finger. This is how I play these chords and is only a suggestion that you try them this way.

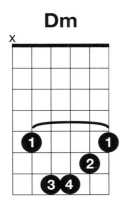

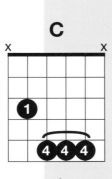

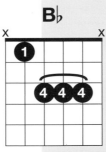

ALBERT LEE

RHYTHM & SEQUENCE TRACK

Sweep Arpeggio

ROCK ARPEGGIO CHORD RIFF IN

D

32

A mixture of arpeggios and pedal note chords helps to give this an interesting sound.

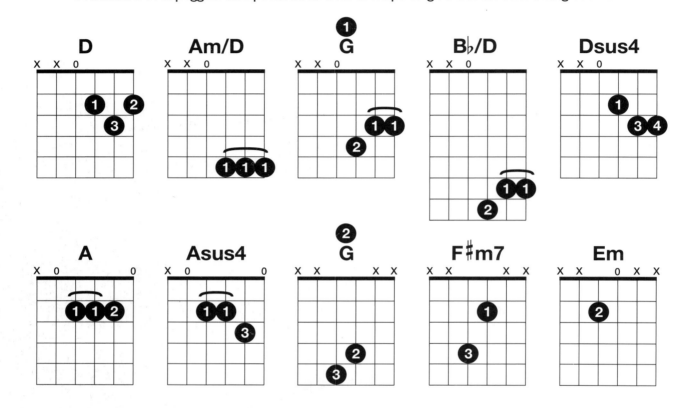

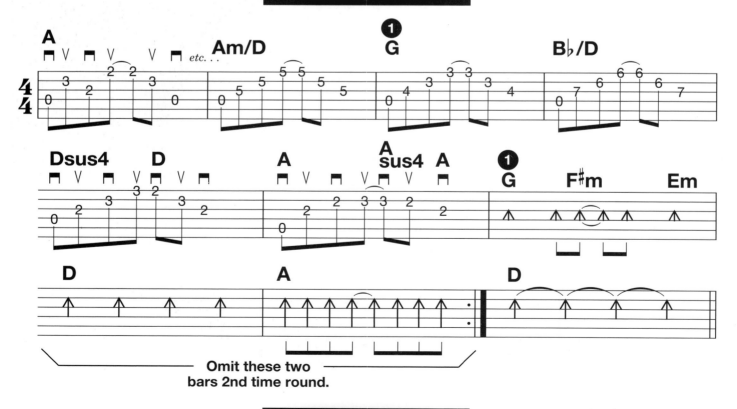

Omit these two bars 2nd time round.

POWER ROCK CHORD RIFF IN

D

This is a loud power chord riff with loads of impact, ideal as an intro.

Dsus4

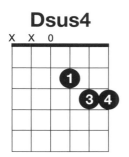

D

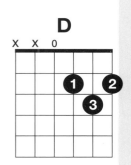

E

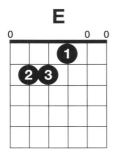

C

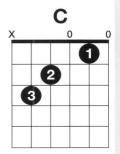

VAN HALEN

RHYTHM & SEQUENCE TRACK

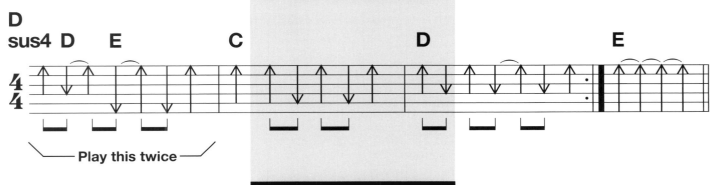

CHORD RIFF IN D

Here is a chord riff making use of the D 'pedal note' on each chord. Watch for the slide in the second bar.

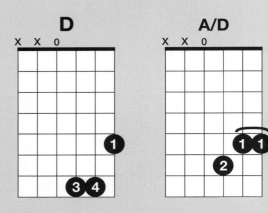

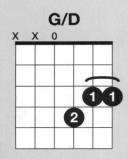

RHYTHM & SEQUENCE TRACK

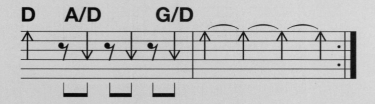

COUNTRY ROCK CHORD RIFF IN D MINOR

COUNTRY ROCK

Tune your E 6th string down to D for a 'deep' sound. (After you have loosened the string check that it sound an octave lower than the D 4th string. Another way is to sound the 7th fret note of the E 6th string and play the open A 5th string, it should sound the same).

RHYTHM & SEQUENCE TRACK

Tune to D A D G B E

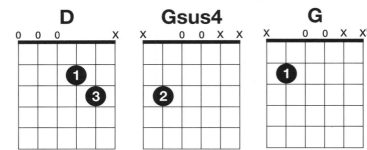

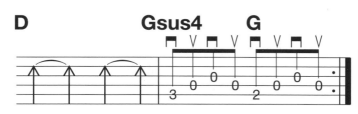

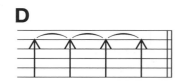

This riff also uses a down tuned 6th string. For the D7 chord in bar 1, while pressing down on the 3rd fret of the 5th string, push the string down slightly so that it creates a string bend. (You will hear it on the recording.)

D

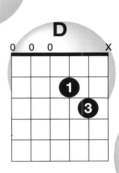

D7

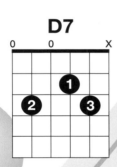

C

❶

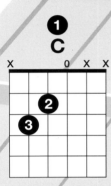

G/B

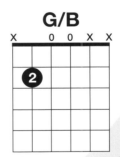

B♭

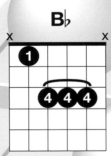

C

❷

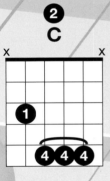

RHYTHM & SEQUENCE TRACK

Tune to D A D G B E

D D7 D   C   G/B   B♭   C   D

Play this 3 times

CHORD RIFF IN

HARD ROCK

37

If you can get a dirty setting
on your amp, use it up full
for this riff.

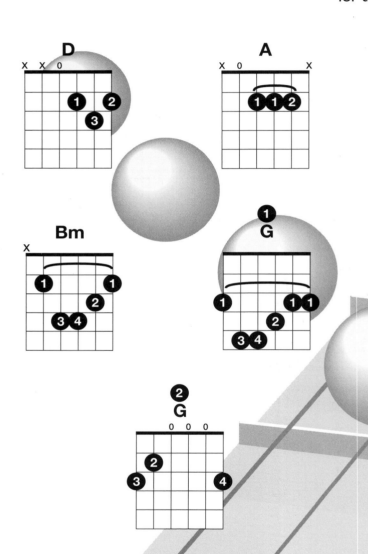

IRON MAIDEN

RHYTHM & SEQUENCE TRACK

38

Power chords, coupled with a slightly funky rhythm
sound great, especially in the chord riff featured here.
Note! Remember the importance of working on the right
amp setting as the actual sound needs to be right as well!

E

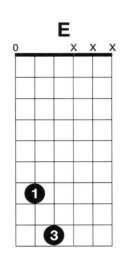

D/E

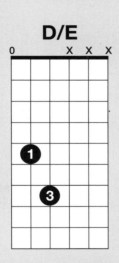

A

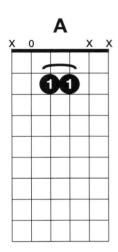

G

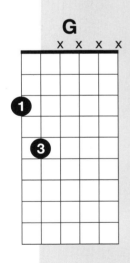

F♯

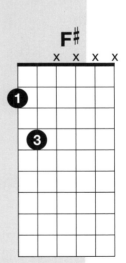

RHYTHM & SEQUENCE TRACK

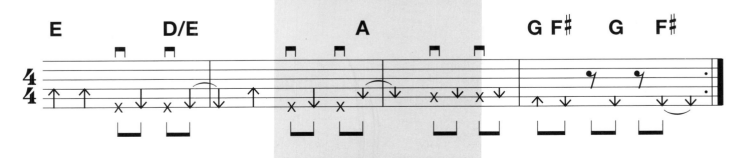

CHORD RIFF IN

39

The root note of each chord (except the E♭ chord) acts as a rising line throughout the riff. (A G bass note is sustained for the root note of E♭.)

STEVE VAI

E
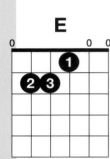

F#
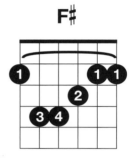

E♭/G
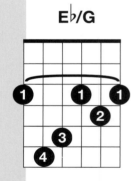

A♭
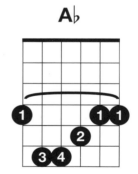

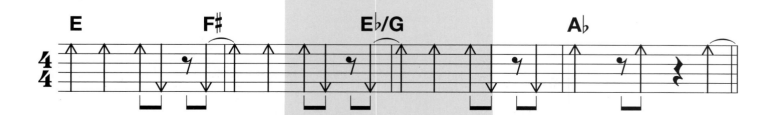

Here's a turnaround that's been used frequently in rock songs and solos. A turnaround is normally used at the end of a 12 bar sequence to bring you back to the start again. Try damping the strings for a 'chunky' effect. This is achieved by lightly resting the palm of your right-hand directly on the strings at the bridge.

E
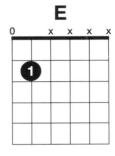

E6
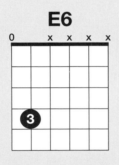

E7
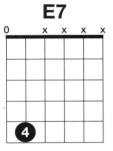

A
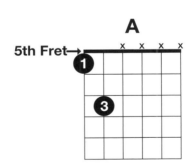

A#
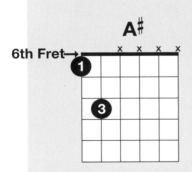

B
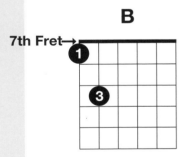

RHYTHM & SEQUENCE TRACK

E   E6   E7   E6   E   A   A#   B

$\frac{4}{4}$

41

With a combination of chords and pull-offs we end up with a classic
hi-energy lead riff used by heavy metal guitar players. Look at the
first position of each chord diagram and you will see a dotted circle
with dotted a number eg. In Em ❶, it is in readiness for the pull-off
note to bring you on to Em ❷. Notice also that you have to
perform a triplet of notes.

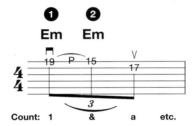

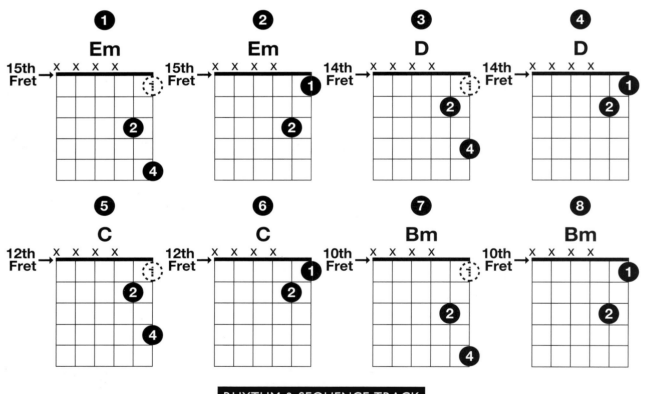

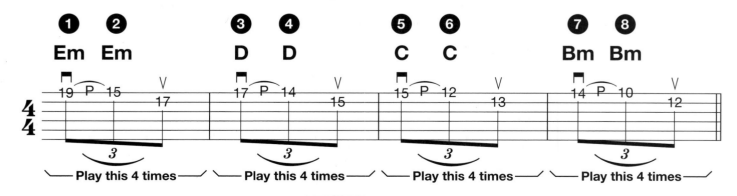

This chord riff has a funky groove to it. With a raw rack edge it can sound quite powerful. Here's the rhythm laid out in basic form.

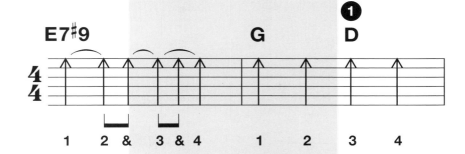

RHYTHM & SEQUENCE TRACK

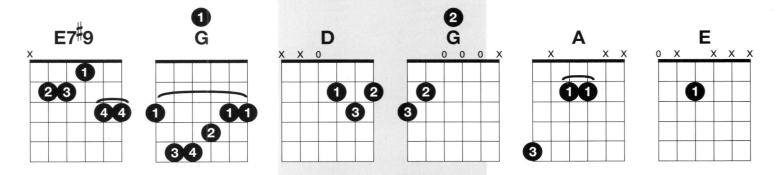

Play this twice

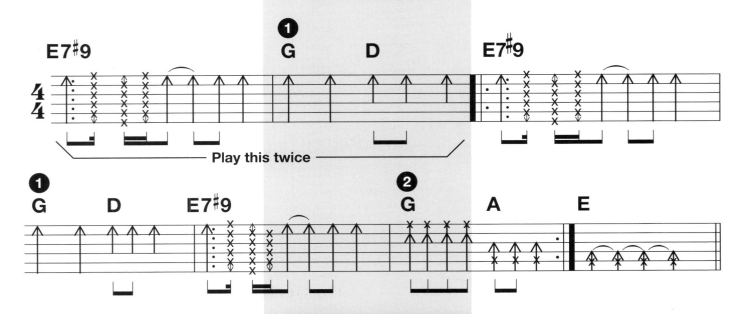

POWERCHORD RIFF IN
E

Here's a really powerful chord riff to keep you on talking terms with your neighbours. When you come to the B chord take extra care when you bar the strings on the 4th fret. I've seen lots of guitar players laying the finger flat so that it includes the 4th fret of the 1st string and it really kills the power content of the chord, so work hard to avoid this. (Other alternative fingers can of course be used to form this chord if you prefer.)

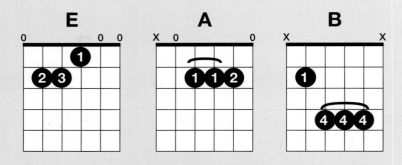

RHYTHM & SEQUENCE TRACK

Play bars 1 & 2 four times

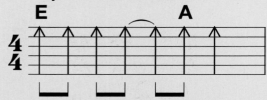

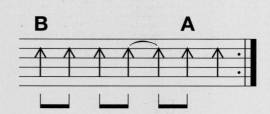

POWERCHORD RIFF IN
E

An easy but effective chord riff using major chords throughout. Just strike each chord downwards.

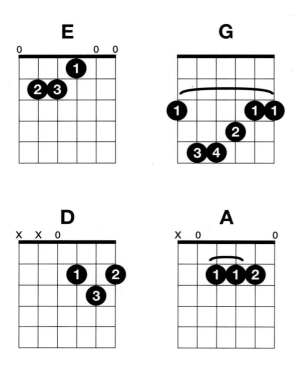

RHYTHM & SEQUENCE TRACK

Play this 4 times

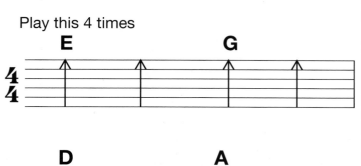

45

Try this rockabilly riff which is rather like a lead break, but using chords instead of individual notes. If you are using an electric guitar and you have an effects device try using a short slapback type echo for a hotter rockabilly sound.

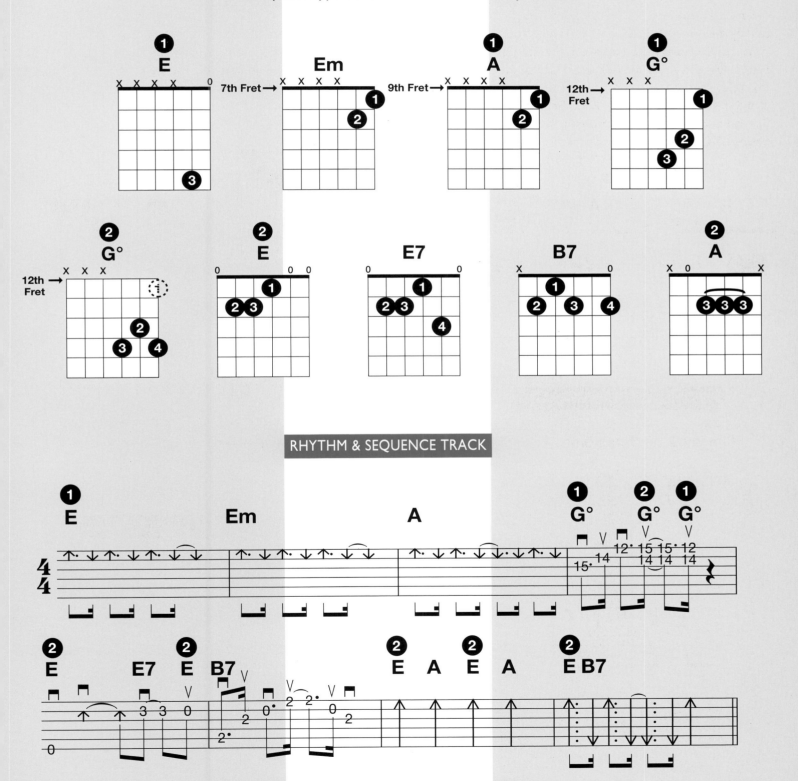

RHYTHM & SEQUENCE TRACK

Here's a great powerful sounding chord riff, you'll need plenty of overdrive on the amp if you can get it. You must try to change cleanly from chord to chord. Try bringing the volume up on the last chord for a more dynamic effect.

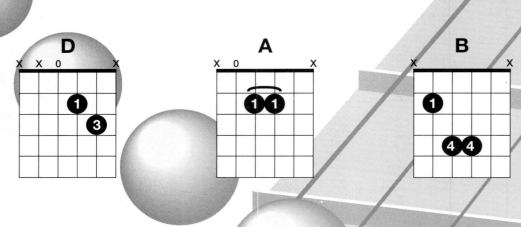

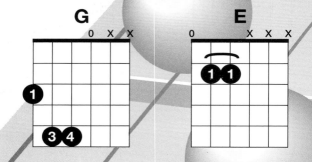

RHYTHM & SEQUENCE TRACK

Volume Swell

CHORD RIFF IN

ROCKABILLY

Try this with a slapback echo effect if possible.

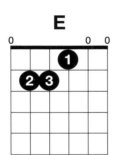

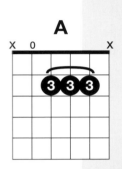

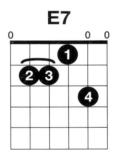

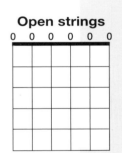

EDDIE COCHRANE

RHYTHM & SEQUENCE TRACK

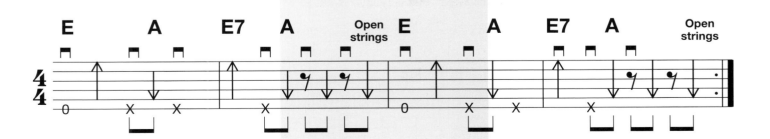

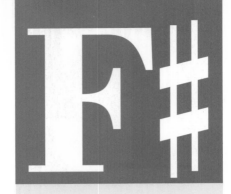

48

It is important to make sure you only sound the 3 notes from each chord here. Try laying your 'free' fingers lightly across the unwanted strings to deaden them, then you don't have to worry about hitting the wrong notes with your right-hand.

F#
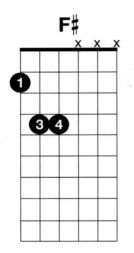

A
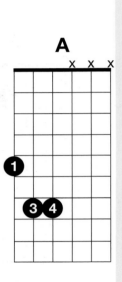

B
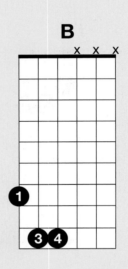

E
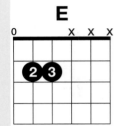

D
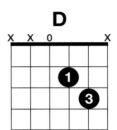

RHYTHM & SEQUENCE TRACK

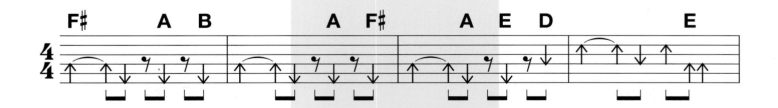

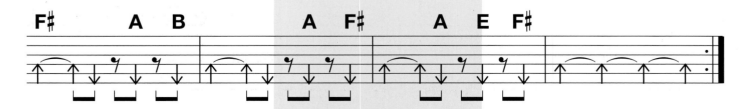

G

When playing this chord riff make sure that when you form the Dsus4 chord you have your 2nd finger on the 2nd fret of the 1st string (look at the diagram) ready to pull-off onto the next chord which is of course D.

G

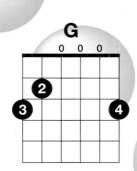

Dsus4

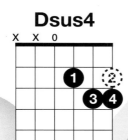

D

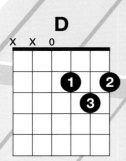

Open strings

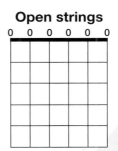

C

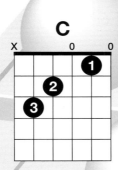

Cmaj7

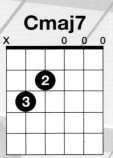

RHYTHM & SEQUENCE TRACK

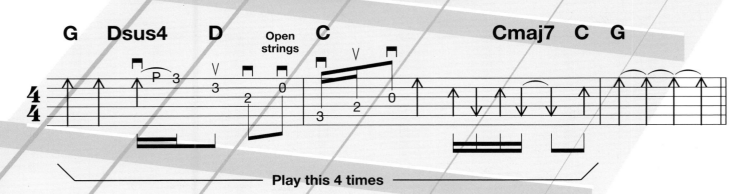

Play this 4 times

The basic rhythm for
this chord riff is

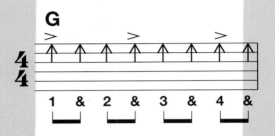

(Try counting 1, 2 and 3, 4 and
accenting the marked beats (>) before
playing the complete rhythm pattern.
Keep going over this until you're
happy with the feel.

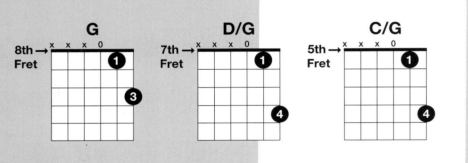
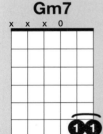
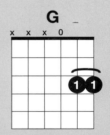

RHYTHM & SEQUENCE TRACK

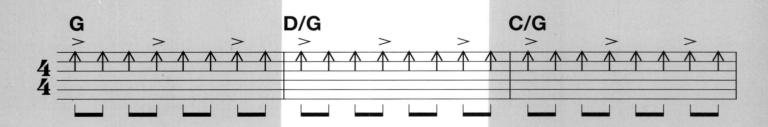

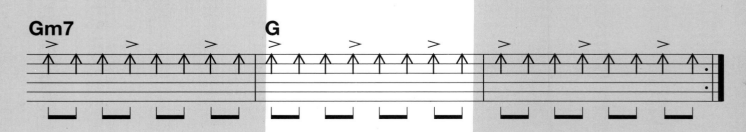